Osmosis

Osmosis

Debarshi Mitra

HAWAKAL

hawakal

Published by Hawakal Publishers
185 Kali Temple Road, Nimta, Kolkata 700049
India

Email info@hawakal.com
Website www.hawakal.com

First edition June, 2020

Copyright © Debarshi Mitra 2020

Cover image: Shutterstock
Cover design: Bitan Chakraborty

ISBN: 978-81-945273-3-6

Price: 200 INR | USD 9.99

Acknowledgments

I would like to acknowledge the magazines and their editors in which these poems first appeared. "Airport," "On Arrival," and "On a Winter Night" appeared on the *Coldnoon* e-zine. "Climax" and "Distance" first appeared on the *Scarlet Leaf Review*. "Prelude," "Spectra," "Pensieve," and "Rain in the city" first appeared on the *Queens Mobs Teahouse*. "On a rain drenched morning," "Three Things," and "Reading between the lines" first appeared on *The Sunflower Collective*. "Palimpsest" appeared on *The Pangolin Review*. "Dream" first appeared on the *Esthesia*. "Loss" first appeared on the *The Lake*. "Portal," and "Hourglass" first appeared in the *Thumbprint Magazine*. "The Lake," and "14/4/20" first appeared on *The Seattle Star*. "Elusion" first appeared on *Poetry Online*. "Dawn" first appeared in *The Indiana Voice* journal.

Introduction

This thin volume contains 35 poems. The collection attempts in various ways, to crystallize and observe 'the moment' and to sublimate it through language. This impulse stems directly from my curiosity regarding Zen Buddhism and formal training in Physics. Even to the most unimaginative of Physics students it soon becomes evident that what is seemingly ordinary is quite often not so and is merely a manifestation of intricate, inscrutable mathematical formulations. Having said that, one also gradually begins to realize that Mathematics like language itself is an abstraction, a way of describing in a self-consistent manner all that is observable and tangible.

It is in this vein that the book was conceived. The attempt was to de-familiarize the ordinary by not resorting to obfuscation or embellishment but merely by revealing or portraying it with as much clarity and transparency as is possible. The mundane in my opinion when looked at with a gaze that is unflinching and refined can open up new spaces and lead to a deep and suffused silence.

This can often be experienced in the works of several Imagist poets or Haiku in the Japanese tradition where images give way to a larger sense of freedom and vastness. The 'moment' becomes absolute and all encompassing, the self having been merely subjected to time's passing all this while, can now for an instant stand outside it, with its presence now diffused. Thus poetry can often be liberating not just in a social or political sense but also in a more profound existential sense. The transformation of the observable and the familiar leads to a widening of perspectives, tranquility and   profound sublimation.

This is however not to say   that the manuscript achieves all this. On the contrary in my opinion the manuscript has failed on all counts. However poetry, which to me primarily is a means of communicating immediate experience is an exercise in failure. One writes because one is compelled to. That is all there is to it. The book was compiled over the last five years and was conceived as a way of stepping aside to simply exist, away from the incessant information overflow of social media with its repeated self-aggrandizement and pseudo socializing/network building and other associated distractions. The attempt was to return to the immediate and the sensory, and more importantly to find equanimity. In an age of increasing commercialization and market mediated identities the aesthetic choice of minimalism and sparseness perhaps is a way of returning to the 'pure,' the 'sensory' and the 'immediate.'

Most of the poems included here have been published before in several journals as duly listed in the 'Acknowledgments' section. I am thankful to the editors for their close attention and invaluable suggestions. I would also like to thank some of my friends who painstakingly went through the poems. They know who they are. Since poems, as Celan said, are bottled messages waiting to be found, I hope these poems too will find their readers and resonate with them.

Debarshi Mitra
New Delhi

CONTENTS

Airport

On a barren landscape
falls the shadow
of a metal bird

On Arrival

The air is stiff,
the walls have gathered
cobwebs and dust,
as is expected of course.
The floors have
shoe stains on them.
The bedsheets have developed
signs of neglect.
My books and other things
are exactly where
I last saw them
where they always were,
only my mind

is elsewhere.

Ephemera

In the dead of the night
a raven returns
to her fledglings.
Trapped in her beak
a worm
wriggles in the moonlight
like an unformed dream.

All alone

led astray
by a thought
barefoot
walking
on a winter night.

On a Winter Night

You close your eyes
and draw a blank.
The fog is everywhere
around you.
The past continues
to keep you at bay.
Your dreams begin
to turn yellow
like the flame
of a distant star.

Gestures

The first rays
of dawn travel
through space
and in the restless
shuffling of bodies
the epiphany
of touch
like a thought
gently alights
on the world

and a sense returns
of having forgotten
what was once
treasured, walking
each night through
memory's foggy streets
as the years roll by tracing
the globe's trajectory
in space,
coming undone
by these stray moments
of inertia

while the gears
sputter to life,
while glaciers
gradually melt,
while sleep
visits the eyelids,
while a filament
glows in the dark
like an outstretched hand.

Family Sundays

Anecdotes of
grandparents
and dead aunts.

On the centre table
a decapitated wax turtle.

I look both ways
to cross a one way street.

14/4/20

Outside, the sky
in so many shades
of pink.

Here, a crow
pecking at
the unrelenting window.

On a rain drenched morning

The skies are grey,
the room damp
from last night's rain
and this moss grown house
once again succumbs to memory.

I open the front door
pick up the wet newspaper
while a sudden gust of wind
slips in quietly
like an absent traveler.

Notes to No One

Smog: A metaphor for collective amnesia.

Sunlight : An empty box gift wrapped.

Shadow : The unacknowledged self.

Road: The allure of eternity.

Sky: The mind's endless voyage.

Loneliness :The weight of silence.

Chaos : A blank page.

Melancholy

is a half open door
leading to a landscape
misted with time
turning vapourous
steam from a hot cup of coffee
clutched hands letting go of
speech condensing

into silence.

Loss

It was always this way,
was always a metaphor
built on fragments and
a physical space stretched
by light streaming in
from one side of this endless
corridor. It is here that
I preserve the image
of you bending
to pluck tulsi leaves
from a yellowing tulsi plant,
and suddenly remember that
for all these years now
after your passing,
I have forgotten even
to part the curtains.

Palimpsest

Days stacked on days,
memory on memory.

The morning sky
takes on light.
Someone on
the opposite balcony
sips tea.

A raindrop
slides down
my windowpane.

Climax

Once the body
bent in surrender
its underside bare,
the animal
out of breath
gradually receding
wave after wave
along the shorelines
glimpsed all
in an instant.

Distance

A clear
'pin- pointed' stab

    of that

which lies inarticulate
underneath the waters,

    of that

which solidifies
into ice.

Three Things

The sound
of a raindrop
striking glass.

A single feather
resting
on a leaf.

A shadow treading
on the surface
of memory.

"Into the dusk charged air"

let the poets go.
let their words too pass
from your lips to oblivion.
From sunset to sunset
watch the shadows gather
and speak in muted verse,
these invisible legislators
with their silent acknowledgment
of us right now
being here.

Spectra

You whispered
into my ear
a secret prayer
and the day
so delicately hinged
on seven light beams
fell at our feet.

Portal

On the street
that I've known
for the last decade
afternoon tilts gently
against the shadow
of your absence
smudging the lines
between the worldly
and the otherwise,
melting desire
and melancholy
in unequal measure
forcing us
to submit
to the perpetuity
of small recurrences,
to just be like this
for once
to live one life
and to dream
inescapably
of yet another.

An Insect

trapped between
the two hands
of a clock.

Time becomes
an epitaph.

Amphibian

The scent of land,
the sky
vast and dark,
the shadowed
corners of my dream now
suddenly illuminated
by streaks
of daylight.

Pensieve

On some mornings
you think of rain and
the sky opens up,
turns dark grey,
rain begins with
a single teardrop forming
at a corner of your eye
while your mind wanders
from here to elsewhere
where land ends
and the sea begins,
you watch a raindrop
falling on a puddle
and call it time.

Rain in the City

This right here
the tumultuous downpour
and the slow, visceral unravelling
of shadow and memory.
I'm at the verandah again
watching the street below
watching the world
gather its fragments,
the spilled gutters
and the endless traffic,
while on the sidewalk a boy
sticks out a hand
and asks for spare change.

1/05/20

showers
   all night long,
our thatched roof
   leaking,
on the windows
   of our dreams
poems scribbled
   with rain water.

Hourglass

Do you remember
that old mosque
and the roof behind it
where we once held hands
for the very first time,
and saw evening descend
dream-like across the city
and how,
many years later
in a different continent,
the tip of your pen
returned to that evening
just as much
as the one
in which you left.

Twilight

In your voice
only the faintest
trace of sorrow.

The sun setting
on a shimmering lake.

Elusion

At my window sill
is where the pigeons perch
at the onset of twilight.
Under their wings, at a distance,
I see the city and the hills beyond,
their edges marked by oblique sunlight.
For a brief while, they hold their breath
ready to launch themselves in thin air,
and perhaps time warps a little then
indenting the tangled contours of my memory.
I see them contemplating stillness
day after day , at this time,
catch them dreaming mid flight,
a corner of their eye
holding an unmapped sky.

Between the Lines

Reading
between the lines
is a practised art.
In every word
I write to you
watch if you will,
the pale,
imperceptible shadow
of death itself.

Prelude

Traces of fall,
   the leaves sun dried,
the pond still as ever,
   the afternoon
almost
   eternal,
a bird lonesome,
   the tip of its beak,
probing the meniscus.

Found Prayer

Let my name fade away
but these words
let them rise as if out of nothing
but thin air
and parched land.
Let them speak
as the sky speaks
only in the dialect of light,
let nothing remain but these
let them be.

Dawn

A nameless bird
circles overhead
and then disappears

becomes a poem.

Dream

The dream
has always been this:
by the window
a steaming cup of coffee,
the warm glow of the fireplace
opposite the couch,
an unread book of poems too
on the table beside and
your silhouette
on the opposite wall
leaning against mine.

The Lake

An unnamed bird
skims the surface.

You linger
as an afterthought.

Glissando

Thoughts die slow deaths
and just as easily
resurface sometimes,
leaving no trace
of their presence behind,
a gazelle in motion
watches
the forest trail by
leaving it behind,
irretrievably,
do feet have memories
of the paths traversed?
do wheels?
moving through ghost cities
like a lost nomad
a face, a tree ,
a shadow of a shadow,
images coalesce into spheres,
clocks do not tick ,
somewhere down below
a jellyfish glides
through a meditative blue,
through a familiar smudge
of darkness
a whispered secret
slips between
the pages of your dreams.

Osmosis

Between two eternities
of darkness
the vapour trail
of language.